DOG STAR NOTATIONS

HÅKAN SANDELL was born in 1962 in Malmö, in southern Sweden, but has lived abroad for most of his adult life, in Denmark, Ireland and Norway. He debuted at the age of nineteen, and has since published eighteen collections or pamphlets of poetry, most recently *Ode till Demiurgen* (*Ode to the Demiurge*) in 2013. He is also a translator and critic, and a co-founder of the artistic movement known as Retrogardism. He has received several major Swedish awards for his poetry and essays, and selections of his poetry have been translated into German and Hungarian.

BILL COYLE teaches in the English Department at Salem State College in Salem, Massachusetts. His poems have appeared widely in magazines and anthologies, and his collection *The God of This World to His Prophet* (2006) won the New Criterion Poetry Prize. As a translator from the Swedish he was awarded a fellowship from the National Endowment for the Arts in 2006. He lives in Somerville, Massachusetts.

HÅKAN SANDELL

DOG STAR NOTATIONS

Selected Poems 1999–2016

Translated by Bill Coyle

CARCANET

First published in Great Britain in 2016
by Carcanet Press Limited
Alliance House, 30 Cross Street
Manchester, M2 7AQ
www.carcanet.co.uk

A CIP catalogue record for this book is available
from the British Library: ISBN 978 1 78410 184 8

The publisher acknowledges financial assistance
from Arts Council England.

CONTENTS

from Beginnings: A Childhood in Twenty-Two Poems

from Sketches for a Century

from Golden Days

INTRODUCTION

It was late, and Oslo was cold, icy, treacherous underfoot. Håkan Sandell was showing me around his adopted city, and we had just visited some of the more illustrious graves in Vår Frelsers Grav-lund (Our Savior's Cemetery), Ibsen's and Munch's among them. Small votive candles had been placed in front of a number of the graves. Munch's had several, as did the monument to the poet and activist Henrik Wergeland (1808–1845), erected by Swedish Jews in 1846 in gratitude for his efforts to open Norway to Jews fleeing persecution. The cemetery was pitch-black aside from the candles at scattered graves, the moonlight, and the reflection of the moonlight off ice.

During our tour we passed the cemetery chapel where the Russian Orthodox Church in Oslo holds its services. Sandell had occasionally attended Liturgy at the chapel, and I had become Orthodox the year before, back home in Boston. He had thought about converting too, he said. His problem was with one question posed in the ceremony: 'Do you renounce Satan, and all his works, and all his worship, and all his angels, and all his pomp?' To which the expected, and obligatory, response is, 'I do renounce him.' 'Do I really', Sandell asked plaintively, but with a smile in the corner of his mouth and a (what else to call it?) devilish twinkle in his eye, 'have to renounce *all* his works and pomp? Couldn't I just renounce the vast majority of them?'

The problem, or rather problems, of evil (they are legion) are of perpetual interest to Sandell. His work is often spiritual, some-times explicitly so, though it is more often Gnostic – in the good old heretical sense of the word – than Christian in an orthodox sense. The Gnostic strain is a vital one in Swedish poetry, thanks not least to its importance to Johan Erik Stagnelius (1793–1823), arguably the country's greatest poet, and Sandell is the most distinguished contemporary representative of this strain. It's not for nothing that the title of his most recent book is *Ode to the Demiurge*. The struggle between two visions of the material world – on the one hand, as in Neoplatonism and other theosophies, a symbol of a higher, spiritual reality, on the other a prison of the spirit – is present throughout the work, most explicitly in poems like 'The Bogomiles...' and 'The Trash Pile'. For an instance of sympathy, however grudging, for the devil (for one particular devil), I refer the reader to 'The Evil One'.

These are not just big issues, but weighty ones, as we say, and in Sandell's poetry they have real physical heft, occupy a real space. As the titles suggest, the arguments for Christianity contra Buddhism in 'To a Female Friend Travelling in Thailand' and to 'Words for Justyna on Her Departure for a Retreat in Tushita' are advanced in the context of love for the women addressed – for their souls and spirits, yes, but for their bodies, too – this within a symbolic framework that reconciles inner and outer, spiritual and material, and in which our imperfect world, in the Kabbalah *Malkuth*, the lowest *sefirot*, nonetheless contains the loftiest possibilities. Levels of reality are experienced simultaneously in Sandell's poems, as are epochs of time. The narrator of 'The Assault', in the midst of a street fight in contemporary Oslo, finds himself and his opponent participating in the Passion of Christ.

The cover of Sandell's 2003 collection *Oslo-Passionen* (*The Oslo Passion*) is graced by a sketch of the three sorrowing Marys beneath the cross by the Norwegian artist Trine Folmoe, and it was this image that first drew me to the book when I ran across it in Stockholm, in the *Akademibokhandeln* on Mäster Samuelsgatan, in August of that year. I was there browsing the bookshelves more out of a sense of obligation than with any real hopes of making a find. Most contemporary Swedish poetry after Tomas Tranströmer left me cold. Some was high minded gibberish *à la* L=A=N=G=U=A=G=E poetry (or *språkmaterialism*, as the Swedes call it), some was social realist plodding, much simply struck me as aniemic – too many short lines, too much white space hinting at a significance that the poet had foregone the hard work of articulating, too little *music*. Above all it was the music I missed. For that, it seemed, one had to stick to the canonical classics, or head to an *antikvariat* for out-of-print volumes by the score of fine poets brushed aside when Modernism swept the field in Sweden. Still, one never knows. I opened the book, flipped through it, paused at one of the shorter poems, 'To a Mountaineer':

Now all this talk of love's left you fed up,
and you make light of all that tethers you.
Now when you're planning to ascend Mount Kenya,
and mountain climbing's your *raison d'être*,
and to relish the refreshment in loneliness.
But gliding past the steep wall of the cliff,
the line whistling down through the descenders,
and your foot grasping at the empty air –
if then love suddenly should find you there,
you hang, then, by a thread of your beloved's hair.

This didn't speak to me, it *sang* to me. And brief as the poem was, there was an amplitude to it that was invigorating. I bought the book and spent the rest of the afternoon and evening acquainting myself with the poet who seems to me one of the most gifted poets writing in Swedish today, and the most distinctive.

As a Swede living in Norway, Sandell is, geographically at least, on the periphery. This is nothing new for him. Born in 1962 in Malmö, in Sweden's southernmost province of Skåne (Scania), he grew up in the most ethnically diverse city in Scandinavia, in a region that prides itself on its close ties to continental Europe. Along with Clemens Altgård and Lukas Moodyson (who would later find fame as the director of films like *Fucking Åmål* and *Lilja 4-ever*) Sandell was a member of *Malmöligan*, the Malmö Gang, a group of young poets who gave a series of chaotic readings and defined themselves in opposition to academic poetry in general, and in particular to the poetry scene in Stockholm. Northern

Irish poets like Heaney, Mahon and Longley were among their models, poets from another periphery whom they saw as having bested the establishment in London. Asked to leave university after his unauthorised borrowing of an Old Icelandic manuscript, Sandell received an informal poetic education from older poets and fellow *skåningar* like Göran Printz-Påhlsson (1931–2006) and especially Jan Östergren (1940–1999). Both men were important translators as well, and Östergren accomplished the considerable feat of translating much of Hugh MacDiarmid's *A Drunk Man Looks at the Thistle* into *Skånska*, the heavily Danish dialect of Skåne.

In 1995 Sandell and Altgård published *Om Retrogardism* (*On Retrogardism*), a book comprised of two long essays in which they argued that poetry had become too insular, and, in the case of much postmodernism, too contemptuous of its own medium, to communicate meaningfully. For a remedy, they proposed a return to techniques and genres that modernism had rejected or neglected. In the beginning, anyway, Sandell's version of Retrogardism included a strain of primitivism, drawing inspiration from Robert Graves's *The White Goddess* and imagining an updated application of the techniques of oral literature – collective composition, the use of fixed epithets (think Homer's 'rosy-fingered dawn') and a common cache of images. He placed great stress on metre, too, and on its close connection to poetic inspiration. The new poetry he imagined would be at once *popular* and *orphic*: primitivist, but hardly primitive. One of the alternative labels to *Retrogardism* that Sandell and Altgård considered was the one they had used for several years in Malmöligan, *Nybarock* (Neo-Baroque), roughly equivalent to *New Metaphysical*.

Sandell's relocation to Oslo in 1997 was prompted by his encountering there a group of figurative painters – many current or former students of Odd Nerdrum – who were reviving the techniques of the old masters. In his new home Sandell became an important promoter and theorist of this school of painters, and a mentor for younger Norwegian poets who came to him for instruction, principally in metrics. In his turn he was influenced by the painters and began, as he describes it, 'trying to manufacture poems in what I thought to be similar ways, to use in poems something like the monochrome backgrounds of late gothic/early renaissance portraits, or to change the all-too-personal lyric by including dramatised group scenes as in Italian or Dutch Mannerism'. Through his students, meanwhile, he was reintroduced to what he characterises as the 'classicist modernism' of poets like Brodsky, Heaney, Walcott and Milosz. His Retrogardism became less primitive, more classical. *Midnattsfresken* (*The Midnight Fresco*, 1999), the first book that Sandell published after moving to Oslo, marks the beginning of his poetic maturity, and it is the first book from which I have drawn for the present selection.

For some time the working title of this book was *The World That Opens*, a phrase from 'To a Child Two Weeks Overdue', in which the poet tries to convince said child not to delay any longer, that the world, sight unseen, is worth joining. Sandell himself was never entirely sold on the title, and I eventually came around to his way of thinking: it would have centred the book too definitively on his most optimistic, least ironic, poem, and might have seemed to trivialise all the doubt and loss that the reader will in fact encounter in the pages that follow. Still, I can't quite let that phrase go. There is a great openness, a generosity of spirit, in Håkan Sandell's work. Even the saddest and angriest of his poems tend toward praise. There's a stylistic generosity, too, everyday and vatic diction, high and popular culture, modern and ancient technologies jostling amicably in poems that take the time and expend the energy to do their subjects justice. Now, having said that, it's time for me to get out of the way of the poems themselves. As the poet assures the tarrying child, 'the sun and moon will be waiting for you there'.

ACKNOWLEDGEMENTS

Many of the translations printed here were published in their original Swedish by one of two publishers, Wahlström & Widstrand and Mikael Nydahl (Ariel), to whom grateful acknowledgement is made. The translator would also like to express his appreciation to the National Endowment for the Arts for a 2010 Translation Fellowship, which has been a great help in the completion of this collection.

Translations in this collection have appeared in the following publications: *Ars Interpres*: 'The Pigeons', 'To a Child Two Weeks Overdue', 'Soul After Death', 'The Evil One', '*Nature Morte*: iv. On an Eggshell', 'Time and Space', '*The Bogomiles…*' *Circumference*: 'To a Female Friend Travelling in Thailand', 'The Trash Pile'. *Curator Aquarum*: *In Memoriam Regina Derieva* (Ars Interpres Publications): 'Words for Justyna on Her Departure for a Retreat in Tushita'. *The Dark Horse*: '*from* Stanzas to the Spirit of the Age' and 'Xmas. Kruse Street, Oslo.' *Modern Poetry in Translation*: '*Clear sighted? Certainly they were…*', 'Closing Time and Clean up', 'Identity', 'Spring Evening. Shipping Out.' *New European Poets* (Graywolf Press): '*Nature Morte*: iv. On an Eggshell'. *The Other Side of Landscape: An Anthology of Contemporary Nordic Poetry* (Slope Editions): 'To a Child Two Weeks Overdue', 'Soul after Death'. *Poetry:* 'Your Hair of Snakes and Flowers', '*Poetry rejoices…*' *PN Review*: '*Alba: Morning Song…*', 'After a Quarrel', 'Autobahn', 'Ice. Darkness.' '*I don't tolerate alcohol so well any longer…*', 'Requiem for a Returnee', 'To a Young Lady Hit by a New Year's Firework', 'A Summer in the Hood: i & iii'. *Structo*: 'Sketched in the Margin. Oslo in June.' *Two Lines*: 'New Jeans'. *Two Lines Online*: 'Notation'. *Words Without Borders*: 'Twenty-two things *not to be trusted...*', 'To a Young Man Who Arrived at the Party Dressed in a Lady's Fur'. *World Literature Today:* '*Let's say Courbet...*', 'The Assault'.

I owe debts of gratitude to Håkan Sandell for entrusting me with his work, for his unfailing generosity and patience in responding to my sometimes halting drafts, and for his hospitality and friendship; to my friend and fellow poet and translator Len Krisak for casting a keen eye on the manuscript in its final stages; to my wife Cattie for introducing me to the language in which Sandell wrote the poems; to Michael Schmidt for publishing many of these translations in *PN Review,* and for agreeing to publish the present book. Special thanks are due to Helene Knoop for permission to reproduce her painting *Summerbreeze*, which adorns the cover of this book.

THE MIDNIGHT FRESCO

Midnattfresken, 1999

Time and Space

My time is now, my place is here,
the password has long since been spoken –
I don't need to find it anymore.
But like a wing that tests the atmosphere
the eye has trouble searching out a stronghold.
It hurts itself on every kind of trash,
on all things mediocre, unappealing,
clumsily constructed, narrow:
is scraped and battered, slams into the ceiling
and blinks a little in its bruise
until – bend backwards, now! – it rises
and takes its freedom in a widened hall
as if intending to annex that space.
There's only so much one can take
of closed rooms and near suffocation.
Easy to lose the power to create
and crouch down, though the heavens generate
ceaselessly new frescoes overhead
with clouds so airily monumental
they leave behind small remnants
of the blue that consecrated the place.
My eye dies out in your apartments,
grows grey and crowded, the world fades
and only flares up in a lighter's flame
in the instant right before the smoke's new grey.
The roof is low, and I'm a caged creature;
a hasty glance, nothing left to lose.
Treason, I know, to turn my back,
but I fled, out into nature,
to Norwegian mountains, Irish rivers,

and drenched myself in wildest ecstasy;
songs and rejoicing, my head seemed borne along
as on the waves of a strong flood
but an uproar that goes into one,
gaining a foothold, or out into the woods
must one day faithfully return.
The principle in question is still freedom.
They crack my shell but not before the kernel
is ripe, so golden, sweet and perfect
it no longer needs its shell's protection
I feel what I have always felt:
the powers that labour to annihilate
precisely balance out those that create.
And if some kind of task remains, it may be
to fit around the emptiness
something that recalls a casting mold.
I give form and relief back to the dusk,
from the stubble blue I want to make
a colour print that will preserve the time,
a weight for that which hovers, substance
to fill in what is quarried out and hollow.
Sometimes from these grey quarters, comes – although
this doesn't happen every day – an artist
who with the sharpness in a pencil's point
can give a clearer contour to the clouds
and with a few deft lines recreate space
where in the evening – like a god –
unasked, the blue air fills it graciously.

The Pigeons

Healthy metallic-bright pigeons
born in the shadows of forests,
weak despite colourful armour,
silken scarves billowing brightly.
Delicate scarlet feet, perfect
feminine talons, exquisite,
too, on the male of the species.
Heartbeats expressed as attire,
throats curved and slender as serpents',
sea colours far up in fir-trees,
seek me out now after decades.
Hardly-heard tones to the present,
notes on diminutive tongues find
greatness at last in the memory.
Pigeons in shadowy pine-trees
when ecstasy shifts into clarity,
amber-red eyes with night-vision.
Also where you lay broken,
leftovers hawks left in clearings,
fluttering shards of grey opal
weighing the wind down, the forest
stood like a temple around you.
Wings that the waters reflected,
gracing the air and the sunlight.
Meetings with you as anathema,
pollutants, unsuited to fertilize
verdure that sang in our eyes, once,
chased along over the sidewalks
leaving irregular circles
scratched with your feet's curled deformities,
give back an image of purity

rinsed in grey, grape-tinted clusters
trampled down there by the corner.
Lines that recall Leonardo's
are quickly worked over by footwear.
Soot-covered pigeons are reddened;
even in death they are blatant obscenities.
Pigeons that foolishly wobbled
in circuits from dinner to danger;
spat-upon, thread-bare and clownish,
resigned past the point of timidity,
more locked than the flame of a candle.
Yet there is in the pigeon's blue highness
cast in the form of the shadow
of a statue of horse and rider
or, when its wings are extended,
a symbol of gossamer visions,
a hint of its earlier existence
nurtured in a world not yet worthless
when it lived in the forests' dominion.
Less refined minds will continue
to consider it litter and vermin –
are pigeons still able to fly, even?
If sometime you happen to see them
sickly and slovenly, sitting
dour in the gutters of rooftops,
close beside eggs that lie rotting,
you will see plainly a place where
a lustreless poetry flares now and then
in memory of all of its losses.

THE OSLO PASSION

Oslo-Passionen, 2003

The Evil One

for Elena Shvarts

Little enough at first to come in through the keyhole,
as I learned later on, bee-sized, it nonetheless
retained a kind of graceful abnormality when,
full grown at one hand high, its wings spread in a show,
it introduced itself to me with a little nod.
In the dark countenance two eyes as black as coal
cut through the room, body so trim and so athletic
his arched back didn't make him look the least bit elderly.
The creature stood there, black in black as in a rainbow
for the night, smiling, with his moustache's sparse whiskers
trembling in time to the gusts of his sulfuric breath.
'You called on Us,' he hissed, 'you called us with your poems,
their viper's beauty and their underground blue mysteries…'
An elemental? A homunculus? A Nephilim?
I wondered from what ancient race he was descended.
'Do you suppose', he went on, 'you can simply stroll
as you see fit among Our ranks? Well, let me tell…'
The little dark thing on my desk got a good slap
that knocked his golden earring off; he started whining,
praying, imploring – really a pathetic character –
and offering me at the same time power beyond imagining.
The worst was when he started staying up all night
working on drafts of poems and then expecting gratitude.
He complained often: too cold, too damp, and through his chattering
pike's teeth he stammered, 'Someone really ought to set
fire to something, oh the red flames would be magical'.
And then, one winter evening, by accident, he said,
my manuscript burned up, that big, colourful tract
of morning stars and blue-black brier-roses that

the fiend had illustrated but that he, rebellious
as always, turned into a string of oaths and blasphemies.
Time passed, and he grew thinner, and he stopped his nagging.
He shrank and paled, turning more bluish; he began
sleeping all day, while evenings he sat up and fanned
himself in vain with his dry wings, feverish and sweltering.
The skin hung from his backbone like a sail gone slack,
his buttocks, once upon a time grape-blue and tight,
withered, and looking at his wings I could see right
through to the pale arteries where the blood had dried.
I made the little wretch a bed out of a shoebox,
and though he found my sympathy repulsive, I
heard only the occasional obnoxious comment
as I rubbed Vaseline into his wings to try
and ease the awful dryness, and in my hands his long
ears were so chapped and brittle that I nearly cried.
I fed him with a coffee spoon: a sip of bullion,
a drop of rum sometimes; and this although he tried
to clamp his lips shut tight; talk about devil's spawn!
Still, he was company; in the evenings I could tell
that he was there by glimmerings from his direction
like the last hints of light and fire in the sunset.
One morning he lay cold and rigid in his box.
It was a shock; the loneliness came welling up
then, and I wept for him on his descent to hell.
My sorrow was unfettered, wild, irrational,
and for a long time I just left him lying there.
Eventually, I went and burned him and his box
and hid away the pieces of his skeleton
from my eyes' sorrow, hoping, too, to shield myself
from the incomprehension of both foe and friend.
But first, just out of curiosity, I measured
his corpse: twenty-four centimetres end to end.

To a Female Friend Travelling in Thailand

Soon, when your foot treads European soil once more,
and this five weeks since your departure, weeks of sheer torture,
then subterranean electric shocks will go
throughout our Union, on up to my exile's Oslo,
where heart and soil will shake with a volcanic explosion
that breaks the crust and melts like blood all that opposes
the scattered flowers that resurrect themselves and grow
up suddenly among the birds' nests, fruit trees holding
their branches empty from sheer faithfulness, devoted
as no place can be save our hopeless old Europa.
Evenings we put on black, mirrors wear veils of mourning
in bedrooms, and the people here seem gauche and gross.
Since you've been gone, the sick have lain past hope of cure,
the juvenile delinquents go more antisocial,
and, backs turned on their inspiration, most of the poets
incline to striking noncommittal, modest poses.
But tell me, did you find the deep peace of the soul
there beneath aqua skies the sun had edged with gold
with your hands clasped together in an open lotus,
did your 'I' wink out there in that country that extols
the qualities of concentration and composure,
or did you take from the world's dripping claw the flow
of wild blood down the cheeks of young men, from the sold-off
attractions of the women, from game cocks and cobras,
that blood that burns through the illusory world we know?
Or maybe, in the arms of the one you're travelling with,
you've put off choosing either, gold-bronze, oiled up, glistening,
with just the inside of your navel showing snow-white still,
and chilled, refreshing drinks borne out to you, until
those of us here at home seem less and less familiar,

unreal as movements in those rice fields in the distance.
In any case, know that he, too, is loved. And this
I say by way of vindicating your suspicion
that I am an entirely lost individual.
Rather than Buddha's calm, I choose the Crucifixion,
choose love, its fires, rather than desire extinguished,
falling in love, with all its painful probabilities
all the way up from graves' remaining residuum
of friends from youth, little white powders that don't fill
the urns they were poured into. They were killed,
but we're here still.
              When you return, as soon you will,
oh then at Santiago de Compostela, pilgrims
will gather, on their knees, like me, because you are immanent…
I await you like the dealer waits for his big shipment
of 'snow' from dreamland, from the drug's pure spring. Listen,
a touch is the one thing that can deliver me,
the landing gear being lowered, then the landing strip,
you disembarking, then the soft click of your flip flops
through Schönefeld or Charles de Gaulle, and my one wish is
that everything might start again from the beginning,
the continent be salvageable and I with it;
decay, instead of disappearing bit by bit,
reverse and circle back into its genesis,
so that again there comes the swell of hidden rivers
beneath tree bark and feathers and the thin, pale skin.
And if that fails, well, then, if things could just continue
the way they were before, go on with the same pitiless
longing that through ranged years of creativity,
love, self-destruction, neither failed nor found fulfilment.
Europe is in your hands: come home, grant my petition.

To a Young Man Who Arrived at the Party Dressed in a Lady's Fur

When you got to the party, sent by God knows
whom – contingency, probably – wearing only
a lady's fur, at the outset closed,
though only thrown on, shut but unbuttoned,
nothing else on and totally bonkers
like some awesome Saturday night exotic
dancer at the apocalypse, then, implausibly,
the mood softened; goddamned obnoxious,
obviously, but also with a waft of honesty
from your naked lodging in that savage cloak,
soaked in the skin's perfumes and washed
unexpectedly up on wine-soaked coasts,
you stretch and yawn, posing, half exposing,
and half not, your glistening body,
flecks of light from the Venus's shell sticking,
still, to your throat's and collar bone's white skin
pressing against the fur, caressed like the Virgin
caressed the Christ child where he lay hidden,
startled to feel yourself devoured one instant
and the next evicted from the soft interior
of the fur, its seamless, snug abyss,
from nature's brim and from the night's pit,
naked as Joseph when his brothers had stripped him
of his many-coloured coat – but you're going to be king,
already you're the centre of the party, gilded
in admiring glances, young and brilliant,
powdered and rouged, literally tipsy,
the fur half-shut; wonderful, isn't it,
at the same time exposed and cherished so intimately!
You caused us all to remember our beginnings.

The Assault

'Wer hat dich so geschlagen...'

The back catches the initial surprise:
the punch lands – a blind arrow, chances
are, and aimed at everyone and no one.
Tentative small boyish karate stances
searching through the city streets for greatness.
Dispatched, the new initiate advances,
the chorus watching him as they await his
solo there before their semi-circle.
The other punch comes in now from the side,
my left arm moves to block this new attack,
and the right follows up, gliding as lithe as
a cat's paw past his guard to nail him back.
Shock of impact, crunch, the echo widens
like aspen leaves, or cracked limbs, through the pack.
Suffering for suffering I requite him.
Experience is the only thing that teaches.
Now he feels, as though he had gone behind
the world, implacable nearness, his Adidas
warm with the blood and urine pooling inside them
drop by drop, and how it sweeps his
steps along in a transformation, winding
from mighty rivers on down to a drain
where one is nonetheless a part
of humiliation's secret congregation.
So new, confusing, to become acquainted
with how devotedly the body complies,
and over one eyebrow this burning pain.
Remarkable the way one well-aimed blow,
where a benign almighty might well smite
all barriers and let the self just overflow,

suffices to set the unwitting victim right.
Five men behind him – the kid's diminutive size
at night's foot and those fragile features, though,
plus the twitching in his pink skin's tenseness –
I realise that most of all I'd like
to stroke his cheek, not strike him down. I swear by
Samson's blindness, by the lamp that Psyche
glimpsed the naked wing by, Gethsemane
with Peter's sword and Brutus's knife,
I wish that things had turned out otherwise,
and it was without a drop of fury that I
delivered the next – the final – heavy blow.
Is that sufficient grounds, then? To survive
unpleasantnesses? And that any show
of weakness can be fatal? But isn't, finally,
the lamb's life incarnate more sublimely
in the boy's body that lies twitching here
a felled wild animal with the saliva
dripping off of his white, even teeth?
To fall down – Master! – and untie his laces
or kiss his scraped hands would just guarantee
that the next man with his own track shoe places
a dirt star on my forehead, dead-centre.
What does it mean? Was this what was intended,
that the high skull and the brain's tender contents
that with brittle threads wove an identity
should burst like a soap bubble in the end?

On a Proposition

Lovely bumping into you in this press,
our shoulders touching lightly,
yours naked, mine dressed,
and I appreciate your directness
but how, now she has caressed me
through hundreds of nights, could I defect
to you and your one? What sense
would it make to sip from the glass
I've already drunk to the bottom?
Honestly, what could a few
drops of wine more do
when I'm already crazy drunk?
And what could I, torn so deeply
by love that both beasts of prey
and roses have drunk their fill,
have left to give, anyway?
By now I am so sunk in woman
the night is a woman's sex,
warm flesh along my flesh,
her copper hair dazzles me,
and milk spills across the starry heaven.
What could you ever add to that?

To a Mountaineer

Now all this talk of love's left you fed up,
and you make light of all that tethers you.
Now when you're planning to ascend Mount Kenya,

and mountain climbing's your *raison d'être*,
and to relish the refreshment in loneliness.
But gliding past the steep wall of the cliff,
the line whistling down through the descenders,
and your foot grasping at the empty air –
if then love suddenly should find you there,
you hang, then, by a thread of your beloved's hair.

To a Young Lady Hit by a New Year's Firework

A swim in the sea of people doesn't seem to me
too much to ask, really; for once to just let go,
join something bigger than yourself; soulless flow
out of your little form, regress, and simply be—
be what? just be, the stillness in the storm, the foam's
kiss with other foam, otherwise not good enough;
champagne foam – lightly on the wild, steep waves borne up,
through the stream of people, up to heaven's dome,
a drop expired in the ocean, selflessly drugged,
in the delight of liberation and suggestion.
You think so, that to crawl painlessly from your skin
is something to be wished for, I'm just wondering,
to take off, slip out, hear the pack howl for an evening?
In you who come and go with a lioness's freedom
and never learned to dive in anonymity,
that skill is lacking; out of the thousands of like-minded
among that mass's destitute and *nouveau riche*,
it figures heaven's finger would be able to find you!
You really do stick out, with your high forehead – whiter
than haloes, than the pearl light that the moon spins nightly –

it's like you're holding up a target, after all.
People stare upwards, dazzled, sunken in hypnosis,
and heaven rises, also when its firelight trembles
in the pale stars above snow-covered dark blue ridges,
self-renewing in tight intervals.
With all eyes fixed upon the visionary sky
nobody sees the string of blood beside an eyebrow
trickling down, and nobody sees how you fall.
The crowd thirsts after heaven, but to die for it?
– No, maybe they're not really THAT on fire for it.
In which case heaven really only has eyes for you,
and being chosen is no choice – the clock strikes twelve,
a cheer goes up, but no one sees you where you lie,
on the border between revelation and mere weakness.
You sprawl there like an angel who has been laid low,
shining despite the fall, pale in your bed of snow,
with the blood angling down along your high cheekbones.
Can hazard's god be unconcerned with beauty? No,
he's music, he's approval, but he isn't blind.
Or was it just the sharp point of this empty heaven
that sought you for involuntary coronation?
A crown of thorns over your shoulder-length blonde hair,
a bolt of lightning thrown, burn sores here and there.
You notice how it stings, must have lost consciousness,
back to life like one who has perhaps seen God,
albeit in all his randomness and approximation.
How could you be the one? you ask. How could you not?
One in a hundred thousand, like love, the odds the same,
the gladness of the many is too lukewarm for you.
For you there is no shelter in the crowd's excuses.
Now you sit here before me, tight-lipped, resolute,
snowy, light blonde bangs fallen past eyes of blue,
tufts like a lynx's, patches where the scalp shows through,
the bandage's white headband and fine embroidery.

Your head – Ah, if I only could have shielded it,
But strong, if fragile, it asserted its uniqueness
in sharp but soft relief, mildly intransigent,
and your eyes concentrating personality
in dark blue irises help make it obvious
that my dreams have collided with reality.
Elite, unique, and now pointed out by heaven's long arm.
You were marked out by heaven, by heaven – remarkable –
can you be seen from there? How beautiful you are?

To a Child Two Weeks Overdue

I realise you may regard me as a meddler,
but if beauty, good will and love ever
wore a human face, it must be your mother's.
She looks so welcoming I have to wonder
if you're not being unnecessarily skeptical.
You're expected, the white, tightly-stretched
blouse where the bra is struggling mightily
to restrain that swelling so as not to overwhelm one
with its friendly generosity ought to be enough.
But maybe she has a lazy-bones onboard, someone
who'd rather stay there in peace and quiet
in that crock pot's lovely, honeyed sweetness
and the magic potion of that rounded crucible
than come out in public, exposed and freezing?
The capsule like a sail, soft and flexible,
vast as the whole world, though a mouse hole.
You stand upright – the sides as smooth as seashell –
and if you decide you want to lie down instead,
you're held as though in a swan's egg. You yourself
are the light where the nights tuck you into bed,

pale star – in ten light fingers
you sparkle, you spin, with head down.
Do you know the secret, just before you spring,
of the world that opens, are you able now,
in that inwardness where the red lips say nothing
to see that when your thin, silken hair
reaches the roughness of her golden brush
the sun and moon will be waiting for you there?
When you've tired of your container's marine
life and the sea swell's untroubled peace
in this, the most feminine of places, and finally
make up your mind to come out in a hurry
you're going to be proud, I know,
of this new being you find holding you.
That despite it all you've come out of the night's
grip to horizons immeasurably broader
will be clear, and when for a time you writhe
beside your mother, as if nothing more than a drop
fallen from the nakedness of her hands or feet,
know that you once again, like a chameleon,
will find yourself in your unaccustomed body.
Brown-eyed, as if taken from the shell of the chestnut,
or blue eyed, trickled from the greater stream,
centre of that milk-scented creation,
naked and newly hatched and perfect.
When from that arch beneath the heart you unwind,
roll out to full length from that fold of velvet,
you'll be greeted by an intimate admiration.
The rounded stomach and the little behind,
fresh from the garden of roses sprung,
how ephemeral, like a cloud, yet how earthly you are.
Welcome, little night-guest, eyes still closed,
loosened from the heavens, rosy star;
like a crèche's Jesus, dreamy, illumined

twenty-pointed, perfect little human,
most wondrous, most beautiful, most linen-soft you,
with the lines of a wave and the skin of a flower.
Come now, come out from your rounded house
don't linger any longer in your corner, in the shadows.
Large in your loneliness, alone in your bowl,
crawl your way out of an outlived world.
The hold can no longer contain your journey
to awakening and the patient completion that waits.
But given how long you've already waited,
you'll probably climb, or so I imagine,
directly up in your mother's lap
and be able both to count and to comb your hair.
Your mum is going to do it all for you,
she already breathes your breath – and nursing?
the little leaves of your hands flutter
on their stems – I swear it – as your thirsty
mouth finds its sanctifying raspberry touchstone.
Like the necks of swans, your arms as you sling them,
thin and fair, around your mother
in a moment of mutual, mild seduction.
Come out for a while – you can always go in
again – I promise you, just like Aladdin
promised his reluctant djinn –
if that embrace doesn't meet with your satisfaction.
Come out, in any case, don't wait forever!
Come out in these years when your mother is young
and believes so hopefully in life's wonder
and that it still can transform everything.

Your Hair of Snakes and Flowers

When I saw one of those men touch your hair,
I heard for the first time in many a year
the ancient battle trumpets and I saw
the banners of an army winding off to war
and felt that blind power urging me to knock
him out with one punch, send him tumbling to the floor.
If nobody had held me back, stopped me,
I would – God help me – have killed him on the spot,
stomped out his blood, and spat in it. I'm sorry,
but you must be aware your winding hair
is different now, a hornets' nest, a snakes' lair!
yes, like a ball of snakes in a flower basket, dear.

Soul after Death

'Now I see clearly that a warming sun
was my body to me and that the converse blackness
of light's abstractions has chilled me through.
I miss the body, and the warmth of blood.
I miss my greying skin, and the daybreak's
cough, the arteries' refilling from the heart
in a strong flood through my autumn colours,
the tattoos as soft as on silken cloth.
In the aged body, in spite of it all,
the remains of youth rejoiced in the present.
The shoulders were worth every bit as much as wings.
A seraphic shrine surrounded the rawhide.
The watch's miniature toy-world on the wrist
contained exhilarating depths in its hours,

the minutes shimmered more than the eternal stars.
I miss the brain's stability – a gem
of clarity, miss the ribcage's breathing,
the cock's hardness, the muscles that tense
in strength, the blood streaming out to the hands
then turning back, as in the crucified man's,
and that the air of what is fine and old and transitory
is able to draw into the lungs once more.
Every scar a precious memory, abandoned,
now, with the wedding ring grown fast to the finger
and the earthly tabernacle so soon wrecked.
If I nevertheless, one more time,
were permitted to step out of the abstract and enter
that flimsy shelter… I long to go back
like the angel Gabriel to Mary's sex,
to the old security of a point to hold fast to
when identity turns away, and in its absence
the empty space is flooded ecstatically.'

Requiem for P. N.

Remembrance? Description? To be loved?
It's all that I can do for you – not much.
Your eyes are white stones washed by the cool
shimmer of a wave, eyes that have spooled
up a thread of twilight in longing for reunion.
Your eyes have grown even more brilliantly blue.
Are you a mere image? An optical illusion?
There's a drop of demon in your angel. I wonder
why it ultimately took so long for you
to find a landing place with me. Funny,

I'm no purer, no better, maybe a touch
less certain… Is it doubt about the world, about others,
about myself, maybe, that made possible your homecoming?
You haunt me like a desolate house where some punk
has spray painted your name all over the walls.
I wasn't expecting you, even in dreams,
streaming through me like water through underground caves,
soft as the cushions in a coffin, your face
borne along by all you could not achieve.
With a strength that surpasses its own, I wonder,
does it carry you along or does it hold you under
in nocturnal darkness with no hint of day?
I can hardly believe you've been rotting in the grave,
your jeans and t-shirt tattered and frayed.
Didn't Lazarus, when he came back, smell awful?
You smell so healthy, seemingly unshaken
by your dark journey, wide awake,
brain undamaged, not some monstrous zombie,
but so pale that your blonde hair glows
the yellow of butter or dried yellow blossoms,
fresh new cloth in your dated clothes.
I don't dare ask questions about the kingdom of death.
Your eyes flashed dark blue with wrath
at having to leave this life already,
your death day present in birth's wrapping paper.
If there's innocence for one who so palpably knew
her mortality – a hard beauty, no question,
yet even here, tonight, I'm attracted
to you, violently, but then the truth
hits me – you're dead, 'I know that, yes',
you answer, in the patient tone one uses
with someone dim-witted one is nonetheless fond of.
You embrace me, your soft round forms
out of the past – you press me to you,

hard, hard, but I can't hold on to you.
I might as well try to maintain my grasp on
a frothing wave as it barrels through
or carry a basket woven out of moonbeams
without spilling any of heaven's blue.
To hold you here is more than I can do.

BEGINNINGS: A CHILDHOOD
IN TWENTY-TWO POEMS

Begynnelser: en barndom i tjugotvå dikter, 2004

Autobahn

A dirty blue, thunder-dull, veined sky,
though in my eyes it hadn't yet managed
fully to turn colours, and I hadn't decided
just what, exactly, had created what –
was the sky flowing forth from my eye,
or was it holding me fast here to life and breath?
The earth was light and new, the autobahn –
a black river came streaming along with us
in the median strip, torrents in the ditches.
Pine trees towering colossal, disproportionate,
and dark painted firs from illustrated stories
though the acid rain's light violence must
have left its metallic hues already.
During stops alongside roads to piss
the forest was silent, among lichen-grey trunks –
the ears of the forest – I saw them – listened
to the sprinkling whisper of our streams
deep in the forest, pale gold as the light.
My father's penis, the dark blue shadow
of a mighty tree branch or a peacock's sleek
curving neck, oh ho, impressed by its size
I looked down at my own flap of skin,
little as a pinky, zinc-white, a Greek statue's.
The dirty blue heaven shone oxidised
above the roof of the forest as we walked back,
the shimmer grew sharper, and when the sun had dried
the rain from the treetops, there stood the colours
of the renaissance in the gothic forms of the pines.

New Jeans

It was a denim strong as the canvas of a sail
bought at the Army and Navy on Engelbrektsgatan,
dark blue and even darker with blood
stiffening the cloth like the ink from a ballpoint
along the narrow hips of my drainpipes.
Just turned fifteen, you right behind me,
a somersault from my bike had torn up the knee,
a sword thrust from the bike's mudguard,
back at your house you had me take off my jeans.
You studied the wound's broad smile
and the blood's oozing little tongue
where it had committed its trespass over the edge.
Gravely you washed it with cotton,
warning me how it was going to sting.
The Salubrin's saline pain and the twinge
climbing all the way up to the inner thigh
so close to your face, and your fingers
so mildly cleaning the dirt from the wound.
Then the bandage over it, and you take the jeans
with you to sew up the hole in the light.
The skin's own delicate embroidery beneath the denim
will soon have imitated your even stitches,
two months more and the summer sun bleaches
both of our dark blue pairs of jeans,
four months more and the whipping wings
of death's nothingness take you under the bright sky,
only the traces of femininity left behind
in the white, scarred wound, soft as a caress

I still bear invisibly from you,
together with a sealed-in mystery deep
in my breast, in the blood-brittle box that only
your little, thread-thin key
will ever again be able to open.

Upbringing

Grandmother describes the river
as she remembers it
once upon a time.
How archaic it was
how fresh and green
washing through the grass
and the roots of the great trees
with crowns wide as the sky.
That's how it was, then, do you see it?
Yes, yes, I see it.
Can you sense how far
it has flowed along,
how strong the current is
that turns the water dark blue?
I see it in front of me.
Grandmother describes the bridge,
small, but well grounded,
she shows me its bow
with one hand curved just so.
That's how it was, do you see it,
and do you hear the wheels of a wagon
on it, how they groan

in their woodwork, do you hear them?
I see ... I hear them.
And when the wagon falls in,
can you feel it,
how cold the water is
forcing in under your clothes,
how it weighs them down
and chills itself deep
into the blood, into the bone,
where it draws you down
in its black deep of dreams?
I feel it, yes.
Only then is she content.

SKETCHES FOR A CENTURY

Skisser till ett århundrade, 2006

Ice. Darkness.

(Ovid, *The Metamorphoses*, XI, 594–596)

Hidden, preserved, a star lying low,
shining in the night, pale white, grounded
as a glacier, of a piece, ice and snow
packed in tight together, surrounded
by stone and shadow and thickened darkness.
A block of salt for Audhumbla to lick,
shrinking, with softening edges, rounded
corners, spotted old silver,
the nights' great, preserved block of ice
resting heavily in the middle of the yard
in this, the darkest of all backyards;
an inland ice that has never drawn back,
thin on the dish left out for the cat,
but otherwise in this giant lard-white slice,
ice-meteor of alienation, Siberian.
Next door's stairwell windows glimmer
from their single panes' iron-edged inset designs
of fire-red and seaweed-green glass in
night wind animated chandelier prisms
chromatic against the spiral galaxy
of the silent stairwell in the amber light,
dangling art-deco jewellery everlasting
in the winter night, yet so frost-fragile
I imagine I were able to cast
a stone through all the years of glass
till the entire twentieth century came crashing
down in a violent sparkling of splinters,
back to the *fin de siècle*, the thirties.
A hundred years of black backyards
in an instant that lasts until the end

of time – that is, till this ice block melts.
They frighten me, these Nordic cities you left
behind you in such a hurry when you went
your way under the same black sky of stars.

Xmas. Kruse Street, Oslo.

Pull up to the table: the ghosts of Christmases past
have joined us, and man, wasn't *that* a weird
winter, snowflakes burning like tears
on cheeks as insensitive, I thought, as a wax mask's.
Because nothing means anything more in the end
than one's empathy is able to mediate, I accept
that poetry has a similar crippled vulnerability,
and joy and sorrow echo in the same instant
in me when I remember that winter's particulars,
the trolleys gliding past the National Theatre,
the empty slope up toward the ritzier districts,
my cheek burning and my brand new city
laid so low by the cold, it was as if it
were utterly uninhabited by women.
Intimacy was something I was unable any longer
to imagine – though I couldn't see what had gone wrong.
But a snow-blue day spun toward the night
before Christmas, and we had a talent for society,
Dimitri with a vodka drink, Jonas high,
Hans buried in military history in the library
again and – perpetually rejected – Lars Daniel
polishing a TV movie, *SS Norway*,
lying beneath the covers with mittens and pen,
resilient as ever, entrenched in himself.
Five men and one woman stuck inside

over Christmas the storyline, christened for a sailboat
snowbound in a driveway across the way,
three of the men, like Lars Daniel, gay,
so there was potential, on paper, anyway,
for a fair bit of action, but in his actual bed
only his pen stirred. Of course he plagiarised
the basic plot from the *Decameron*, but whereas they
were surrounded by the plague, around us lay sheets
of crystalline white for Christmas Day.
My annoying hippie neighbour – but how sweet –
had hung on the handle of the door to my storage
a fruit basket, proposing a Christmas ceasefire
despite paper-thin walls and our musical disagreements.
And now, *Nel mezzo del cammin di nostra vita*
(or: halfway through the journey that is our life),
and so on, only now, when the music's fallen silent
or been transcribed as it were for a higher key
wreathed in white silence, does it strike me that of course
those preposterous Mickey Mouse pyjamas she wore
and the blonde Rasta braids in purple bows
must have enclosed a landscape as warm
and deeply buried in her case as in my own,
as variously branching under unifying snow.

Sketched in the Margin. Oslo in June.

This really is the point in time, this lull,
its softly arched bow like this day's.
I'm afraid – *don't show it* – that it has all
been laid waste, and I'm anxious, and impatient,
if there's time, to repeat the eternal observation

that at least one artist in every epoch
saw flash forth like light from a prism;
afraid that now it's impossible to allow
a new beginning to balance what's been ruined.
Back in the Marxist study groups of our half-dead youth,
under the blue-brown, violet sky of a Malmö winter,
Åke, puffing on a pipe, brooding,
we believed the future was created by the *diamatic*
interplay of forces – so much for that!
Here now is the future, dynastic, biblical,
a future again a fanned out Nile delta
surrounded by the sterile and unlivable,
doors kicked in in the great rush forward.
What would Michael have said about his future
memories? That now, precipitated from the *fluidum*,
they have become dreamless, dusty, petrified?
Waiting in the sunlight's amber, infused
with flies, for what feels like a millennium to be excavated.
And yet it proceeds, the enormous epic
story that is history; the lettering
on the walls surrounding your profiles is all
ablaze in the beautifully sinking sun
where you sit relaxed, leaning against the wall.
The only ocean-blue here is the sky,
the horizon steeply climbing, an early Venus,
or maybe it's a satellite flickering brightly
above us; the planet he loved, a young
dreamer, his arms as thin as yours, you there,
by the wall, with mysterious light brown silhouettes.
June leaks like a shipwreck, summer break,
from an open car door pours heavy metal,
the music having taken a wrong turn, maybe;
in a stroller parked in the shade, a baby
dreams of body-temperature milk

drunk *sans* glass in the balmy weather,
and a bit further off… a little gang
of Ethiopians, dry leaves of fire round their cigarettes,
sitting in the spellbinding midsummer evening
that soon swarms with silence and conversations,
cast out there where you can't touch bottom,
nonetheless bubbling, holding themselves up,
laugh and point, commenting, most likely,
on me, as I observe them with a professional eye.
Leaning back, as relaxed and motionless
as in biblical times and by the sun dressed
in flaming haloes, children of Abraham
in the fire of Pharaoh, with shadows as sable
as blackbirds, but nonetheless quietly chatting
as if they sat in lively green foliage,
as in fact they do, up here in the north.
Like match flames sketched on the wall, adolescent,
nearly ethereal, graceful and dressed
in fire and dried grass, banished
by harsh guardians from the gates of Paradise.
In *café-au-lait*-coloured tunics, embroidered,
over faded blue jeans visible from the knees
down, as if they waded in the dusk.
They've been written with sooty flames, it seems,
sketched with burnt out sticks dipped in
honey or hemp resin, faces golden,
in the group of half-grown boys, a lone girl
also in jeans and running shoes, shawl
pigeon-blue, beside her a Coca Cola,
all of them stuck to the wall, boldly
sketched with soot and linseed oil, all
drawn in the margin of the day's chronicle
on this side of the Radisson's futuristic landing
in the neighbourhood around Rudolf Nilsens Plass,

stranded here from Ethiopia or Eritrea
in the old heartland of Oslo's working class
and this in a truly dark corner of Europe
named for the favourite poet of the poor;
a generation passed, kids worked their way up,
and from dead grey shells the winos crawled,
while the tenements stayed behind, so generous.
And this, just now, is the moment, fleeting,
where you lean back beneath the basketball net,
the sun sinking low, the Coca Cola sugar sweet.

Requiem for a Returnee

Czeslaw Milosz has moved to Krakow,
I heard from his Swedish translator yesterday,
to draw in with a deep rattling breath
the concrete dust by the building scaffolds,
breathed out again as the muse speaks her last.
And yet it seems like the scene of his death
should have remained a California
of perfected loss, peeled, wide open,
trembling with desert heat and alienation,
a well-aged alienation, where not the Beach Boys
but Chopin, Brahms and Shostakovich
are played at the cultivated funeral.
Nicely-built young American female
poets would have sparkled in the backmost benches,
hour-glass shaped after a lifetime of salads,
elegant too in the most stylish clothing
with small straps of cotton over their shoulders,
with that self-satisfied self-preoccupation
I too will adopt any day now
in order to claim my feminine rights.

Paler, now, after the warnings about skin cancer,
for over two decades leanly writing
for no one but themselves or no one
but their lovely, gold-framed reflections.
So cool in spite of the heat, and sexy
like they would be if all of the men had died out
and they were sexy only for themselves and
for the shelves in the lesbian bookstore.
Poets, yes, but more like muses
for fate, music, and watercolour painting.
Muses for sports cars, for the streetlights'
mildness in the dusk, for the blue of the waves
and of the neon letters high as falcons,
they all of them seem to be the bearers of a peculiar
bittersweet inspiration with no one to receive it.
Oh Sappho, California, sweet music,
why does Czeslaw Milosz travel to Krakow
only, at the birth of his country, to die
like an utterly ordinary grey old man
when the long beaches' mummifying heat
and a sea as blue as a white cat's eye
made a background suited to a Greek god,
youthful in jeans and drunk on exile
like Odysseus's men on milk-sweet lotus?

Alba, Morning Song...

Alba, that is to say, morning song,
goddamned early, same old world,
though each new day presents it differently.
Blinded by the light, headache brutal,
sweat dried in, awake in the dawn.
Where have I landed and who are you,

here in the pale grey wrinkled covers?
On steady legs, across the enormous
floor, a room as broad as a ballroom
by your lights, I realise, seeing you there,
a fine figure in my toad's-eye view,
on small round legs, your fair hair
like cotton, or a lamb early in the spring
that the snow has covered in a thin layer;
four-ish, with a gaze as blue as the hero's
in the *Nibelungenlied* or *The Song of Roland*,
as though created to be sung like a babyish
King David; the little legs as straight as
in a suit of armour from the Middle Ages,
I see you from all the way down on the floor
where I lie in the arms, thin and frail,
of your single mother and sole caregiver,
sleeping exhausted by my side.
You lean in over my hangover
with your total future and future triumphs
together with the generation you'll grow and thrive in.
With your bearing and the fine musculature
of your breast, your carved, sturdy thighs,
an apprentice Achilles, Ajax, Hector –
well, apart from those doughy arms of yours! –
you look at me, a despicable stranger
who has stolen your place and your right,
who has come like a thief in the night.
Bringing the sword of your shadow down on me
you gaze on me now, with the morning light
shaped to the contours of your golden face
with eyes deep blue and eyebrows victorious,
you stand illuminated by… unfeigned love,
bubbling with the encouraging laugh you give me.
Oh, good God, what a vision this morning,
I swear I am going to live better, live differently.

Twenty-two things not to be trusted...

(Hávamál, 85–86)

Twenty-two things not to be trusted:
not night-old ice, not a winter in Skåne
with the ice shining and as yet untrodden
to a confidence inspiring *terra firma*.
Not winter in Skåne, not spring in Norway
with Easter Lilies rising through the snow's crust;
never, ever, for Christ's sake, trust
the blonde from the sticks, fresh off the bus,
the bloodied thread in the labyrinth,
or that to every nice girl in a pinch
an angel comes, outfitted like a demon.
Mistrust a bit the empire's balconies,
they have less of a purchase than the piercing
in the snake's tongue; consider: the ice
in that drink in India will melt, consider, too,
that the red smiles and eyes as violet-blue
as the firmament above the Soviet Union
in one of Mikael Wiehe's folk rock tunes
won't always live up to your expectations.
For the young, these valuable recommendations:
never trust the egg laid by the rooster,
or helpfulness encountered at train stations,
doubt the dentist's gold, the wolf's wool
and the assurances of a golden future;
that it's primarily for your own good
that you've been taken in hand, that you can depend
upon your being loved by your enemy.
No, don't believe for a moment in the imperishable
nature of the shining ice, in the spread
wings of Icarus, in a spider's thread,
in Christian charity with preconditions,
in politicians – or the children of politicians.

Poetry rejoices…

Poetry rejoices even if the culture dies,
over the girl with her first electric, how her high,
thin voice, amplified many times
over by the loudspeaker, is like a giant's
in the green grass of the festival site.
Over the fragile bells of digitalis, how they hide
the pistil and the pollen inside.
Rejoices over rain on the Faroe Islands,
over rendezvous on the Champs-Elysées at evening.
It rejoices over Japan, over Korea,
over arts refined over a thousand years –
the art of swordsmanship, or of drinking tea.
Rejoices over the poet, that his heart still beats.

I don't tolerate alcohol so well any longer…

I don't tolerate alcohol so well any longer,
yet I stay here, where Vaterland's old wetlands drain
to the river, and it's well worth it with this combination
to pass the evenings, hashish and coffee
(gone cold) that flush the blood through my brain.
Those years with the children of the night – back then
there were plenty of them – have left me mementos,
a slight trembling of the hand when, outstretched
in only a shirtsleeve, it's reached by the spring breeze
simultaneously fanning the brushed-out hair
of the Pakistani girls in the fair blue evening
where they stroll past fir trees whose lowermost branches

hide the few snowdrifts that haven't melted yet;
late spring twilight, the first stars overhead –
vaguely white – are planets, they seem friendly,
good neighbours – the Pakistanis, Venus, Mercury.
All my adult life in immigrant neighbourhoods,
and I only hope the incense that ascends
from the down-to-earth Vietnamese actually reaches
the billowing hall of heaven and rescues us.
A touch shaky from the coffee, calmed by the hash,
they balance each other, in wondrous evenings
that darken slowly in a gathered stillness,
where nightly to farewell come welling
mild conversations, women's voices, the bells of bicycles.

After a Quarrel

You're too much of a green-eyed snake, sly,
lascivious, to wear a swallow's clothing.
And if you were a stewardess, you'd fly,
at least when you go flying into a rage,
for Satan Air, to some warm destination.
You crush the high-heeled ladies down on the street
like fly legs to make your mascara, lean,
slender strokes to make your different shades.
Montmartre you so scared it had to flee
and hide itself away in the nineteenth century.
You ask what loving you is like as we
drift on among our hotel bed's icy sheets
and my hands, fitted with vein-coloured bluebells
for masts, set sail on an accurséd sea.

The Bogomiles...

The Bogomiles, followers of Bogomil,
snapped the metal in crucifixes,
the wood in them they broke,
fonts of holy water, the water,
all these belonging to Satan,
they overturned and laid waste to.
Light that combined with darkness
no longer possessed the same
purity it did in the beginning
but belonged to the author of evil.
But I love the wood in the trees,
the roots, the branches, the leaves
that drink of light and rain.
Love railroad tracks, the ceaselessly
branching roads of the conceivable,
rejoice over the existence of minerals,
the lead, copper and quicksilver
in the oils of Turner and Rembrandt,
the renewal, the fulfilment, the vanitas
still-lifes, cherry blossoms, sexual positions
imported from China and India.
Love the soul in the infant
returning, love's theatrical depictions,
unreal, deceptive and perishable.
Love ice, fire, their union
in the humidity of a woman's sex,
nights as much as day,
the heart's abysses, black wells,
the light of the baptismal font, and of heaven,
take it all in on the inbreath
of my animal lungs, ecstasy

from the atmosphere, and the heady smell
of greenery, oxygen and decadence.
But shining in front of me nevertheless
stands Bogomil, who took the cross and from it
tore wood, metal and inscriptions
in his longing for the age of the Spirit.

from *Nature Morte*

iv. *On an Eggshell*

The matter's dead, I imagine.
Once, back there in the twentieth century,
I found left behind in my cabin
on the Berlin train, in the cars bound for Poland,
a sucked-out eggshell pierced with
a piece of straw like a ray of sunlight.
Empty and hollow as a ping-pong ball,
rounded as soundly as a silkworm's cocoon,
a little cranium – a mouse's, maybe –
from which someone unknown, a god of fate
or a demon, had sucked out the life
yet left completely undivided
heaven and earth as one in that oval.
As if listening to a seashell that holds the ocean
I listened at that hard shell
to vanished summers, silent tears,
to the wing-beats over childhood fields
of birds, bees and dragonflies;
heard the echo of empty schoolyards

and touched that chalky armour
as if poking at sketches on the asphalt,
those naive pictures' depictions
of the mysteries of the darker sex.
A world preserved and enclosed
behind brittle walls and fully as alive,
almost, as on that liquidated sun.

GOLDEN DAYS

Gyllene dagar, 2009

from *Stanzas to the Spirit of the Age*

xix

I prefer after raucous Saturday nights
to stroll and at the most nudge with my shoe
the shattered glass and blood left after fights,
rather than joining in the party too.

It's early June but feels like fall to me.
I cried on the street, I miss my daughter so.
Autumn wind stirs the leaves, and from a tree
a flock of black birds glares down, sated, slow.

This happy, fjord-side, ice cream-licking scene,
could I decide, would be dark, arctic cold.
Expansive life, a new beginning's green,
like this, for these, proved more than I could hold.

xxi

The little owl of reason slumbering,
my mindless hand finds your high, slender thigh
waiting like everyone and everything
has always done – unmoving, soft and shy.

You seem made for quick changes in long cars
along long beaches, but you disagree:
it's quite enough, the nightly round of bars,
enough, you claim, this downward drift with me,

and if this mafia movie testifies,
you say, to my 'exquisitely bad taste',
there's blood enough, and rainy, grainy skies,
to match the lack of prospects we've embraced.

xxiii

The absolute clairvoyance you enjoyed
when we first met belongs now to the past.
The evening star shines faintly in the void.
The vast expanses we wandered through so fast,

recently rendered green by your green eyes,
look now like an assumption. We might have known.
A summer that was just beginning dies,
dry from the start. And the triumphal tone

of my opening lines is lamentation now.
The river pukes in the harbour, grey and pale,
The lilac flowers have turned tobacco-brown.
No one is to blame for this betrayal.

Identity

His identity was always wandering, and though it
was as a lackadaisical dandy that we knew him first,
the old bottles filled with new wine:
then he was an actor, then half a poet,
later on a mechanic in a motorcycle gang,

though only a minor cog in its design,
then a businessman, then with a (thinning) ponytail again,
appearing in constantly changing shapes.
But when drunk he very precisely with his knife
would carve into his arm his beloved's name,
so that repeatedly, over two decades, it came
dripping onto the table, always the same,
the living letters a blood-red flame
welling from themselves, from the scar of her name.

Clear sighted? Certainly they were...

Clear sighted? Certainly they were, the old
masters of the Netherlands, with air
clear as a glazed sky on a day in spring,
cloud edges whiter than an apple blossom,
the newly furrowed fields clay-blue and hard
and the blank waters like a vampire's mirror,
translucent dawn, the roads just now set out on.
In the foreground, a crucifixion – matter-
of-fact – nails driven roughly through the hands,
there's no denying it, up front, the violence
flat as a TV screen's, the atmosphere
of streets at 3 a.m., the scent of blood
in damp nocturnal chill – and distant news
like flower vases brought in from the garden.
In the background, the near at hand, familiar,
contented day-in-day-out's expectations,
a consequence-free, future-phobic hope:
spring sowing, life lines, love lines, and those pin-sized
figures that tramp along on the horizon,

alien, from the cottage door unseen.
The line of this unvaried landscape level
as though stretched taut behind a charter flight,
with room up top to wallow in the clouds.
A grey that gives the daylight lightning clarity.
Painfully green shoots on lifeless trees,
canals that slumber like computer screens
and the broad sails of windmills, stubby wings
never again delighted by a wind.

Let's say Courbet…

Let's say Courbet, to take just one example,
who painted portraits on commission, landscapes,
might have been anyone, completely average
artist's existence, but he goes and stakes it
all on the Commune, throws away the still-lives,
his path crossed by the rolling wave of fate.
He makes his sketches of the barricades:
there at the top: the fallen, some of them
are hardly more than boys; or let us say
Géricault, who painted saddle horses
as regularly as some artists paint the sea,
suddenly, on Reality's back roads,
sees he has been abandoned with the troops
in the retreat – Moscow in flames not even
visible in the background, only snow,
the trackless snowdrifts stretching on for leagues,
the details of the soldiers' bodies sticking
up through the snow, cheek stubble, arms and kitbags.

History had chosen him for something greater
than a succession of mere workadays,
so I thought, and I saw it all before me
the kernel of morality in art
waiting for me to strip it bare one day.
But nothing happened. Now, in middle age,
I'm waiting still; Christmas Eve afternoon
in half-darkness with heavy flakes of snow,
I watched on my way home a crooked shape
who with a cardboard box in an entryway
was laying down the foundations of a bed;
a big white beard, but with no rubber band.
He said that he was seventy, and that life
passes awful fast, 'as you will see' –
west-country accent in the capital.
On Good Friday, the empty trolley car
with me and – swollen up – a man-woman
with pink nail polish on the cuticles –
a guy, first, I supposed – who took small sips
of nail polish remover and had no plans,
she said, for Easter weekend but to follow
the line in circles, round and round, till midnight,
an extra plastic cup showing through her plastic bag.
And the other day, my daughter's hand in mine,
with all that's struggling now to grow in her
compacted like the oak's drama in its acorn,
she's pulling at my arm with little tugs:
the first of May and there, red as a sunset,
the advancing banners raised against the sky
in celebration of forgotten victories
and underneath them you can't see the footsteps
can't quite make out the heads, all blurred together
in spring rain so thin it's half turned to mist.

Almost eighteen…

Almost eighteen, one autumn night after another
I asked with Arjuna, Shall I go on or not,
O Charioteer? Each time that I consider
the future, my heart spins like this chariot.

In the dark night again, always the night owl,
reading this piece of a poem eight times as long
as Homer's combined epics, shunning the party
for these long lines and their entrancing song.

Dead centre on the plain of Kurukshetra
the chariot's stopped, the opposing armies wait;
Arjuna balks: better to bare my own breast,
he says, than cut down even those I hate.

But to refuse to fight, Krishna reproves him,
is to refuse to live. The waste of war
will of a certainty entail lives ending,
but death's end leads on to rebirth once more.

from *A Summer in the Hood*

i   *The lion's mouth of summer…*

The lion's mouth of summer has gulped us down,
toothless and soft, ragged as an old fyke net,
where, nervous and excited, half the town

wells toward the Centre in the idle quiet
circling the bottom, trapped, though they exude
an air of dignity, or something like it.

Here New Babylon cruises in its subdued
Nordic Social Democratic vein,
so nice to simply glide along when, glued

to underwear by this sticky heat, each shaven
sex is made intimate, the salmon wear
their sleekest salmon skins, and each sea lane

leads toward the evening's summit, mixing there,
the waters turning brackish. Glances stolen:
the foot, as fine-boned as a hand, is bare

in its plastic sandal, black, although the sole is
as light as on Achilles, rosy nails…
The Chinese, tiny, slender and peach-golden

in July's high halls, how briskly they all sail
past in crisp skirts dry-cleaned till they reflect,
hips driving to distraction all the males.

He's nearly cross-eyed, now, the Arab next
to me – The West Bank's crisis as relayed
by his newspaper's breaking waves of text,

those fine, fish-netted calves – but I'm afraid
the evening's going to have to go on without me,
I watch through the glass window the parade

while the old guy grows curious about me:
why I don't head out on the town to try
my luck – a young man shouldn't, he points out, be

just sitting here in a suit like that! Softly I reply
that the future will make major sacrifices
for someplace like this bar where he and I

sit – stained-wood tables, beer at rock-bottom prices
and just the right degree of dampened gloom.
Yes, the future will respond to the coming crisis…

We're in, agree the bent backs around the room.
Beneath the taps, glasses fill with beer:
silhouetted, crowned with foam, they loom.

I concentrate on mine, though I can hear
how Saturday night's distant roaring grows,
a shudder passes through the atmosphere,

a bell jar seems to muffle every toast,
and dampened but distinct, despite thick walls,
the evening's voice, unwritten, undisclosed,

through everything that has been dammed up, calls.

    iii   *My ear is measuring time in drops…*

My ear is measuring time in drops, pain twists
my jaw, and the newspaper headlines for today
reach my optic nerve as through a mist.

It ought to heal, I heard the doctor say.
Ought? That quack – I barely made it here
half-fainting, through the exhaust, to this café,

my tongue stuck to the glass with what little beer
I haven't spilled – no sense of balance – pain
rules my brain's remaining hemisphere,

and from my ear the pus and blood still drain
down along my cheek and throat, space hums,
small silver bells ring. I may go insane

before the morphine he stuck up my bum's
worked out into the bloodstream and fulfilled its
promise. At once my consciousness becomes

light, beach-ball light, car roofs glide past, sun-gilded,
and softly, maternally, the morphine now
retunes the world from dissonant to idyllic.

Blondes in convertibles with the tops rolled down
glide by en route from the beach, the car wheels spin,
their lips are moving but without a sound,

perfect that way, red gloss, bikinis, skin.
The sun blazes, the afternoon glare is stark,
the minutes always putting high bids in

on the present moment, and my collar's marks
of pus and blood have dried, and a wide smile
comes down the street, teeth white as a shark's,

a cellphone at her cheek, a crocodile
on her white tennis top, pink headband, slender.
A secret music swells in me, meanwhile,

and the soft black of my sunglasses lends
a touch of shading to the sun's harsh glow,
and what is happiness but pain that ends?

Like cherry blossoms that the breezes blow,
the young drift on, fastening on all they pass,
along a light blue watercolour tableau

in jackets, t-shirts. I put my empty glass
down, and now, more tranquillised than tranquil,
wander off to the park. There in the grass

on small islands marked out by blankets
long, smooth legs are pleasantly combined
with undemanding literature where languid

co-eds in the July sunshine have reclined,
braless, as many are, in manifestations
of ordered liberty; on a path lined

with trees, bikes are led off like psychiatric patients.
At first I hardly see them, I'm so beat,
among the one-use grills waves an acquaintance,

no, several, the grill hot in the summer heat,
they offer me, so delicate, so fair,
a raspberry as soon as I have a seat,

my pupil tracks as two thin fingers bear
it up to my mouth, I swallow, retch,
gut dry as sawdust. That's enough to scare

my immediate neighbours, not exactly a set
that I belong to, so healthy, affluent,
among new strollers and full, milky breasts,

their conversation's mutual assent,
the sprinklers where their naked children run.
I am a passing cloud on the firmament,

an icy shadow, a blind spot of the sun.

Notation

Baku, Azerbaijan 2006

I see you in this church without pews, stationed
along the walls or at the iconostasis, in sparse bunches,
and I describe you as though I were taking dictation:
the girls tall and slim, the old women hunched,
repeating the ritual in your diminishing parish,
kissing the icons, and thinly, as with the tongues
of birds, praising the Lord Sabaoth, where you were abandoned
by a retreating empire that suddenly reconsidered,
rinsed and scattered like seashells stranded
on a beach, and I recognise, half sacrilegiously,
the situation for the poet and poetry: the context
is long since gone, but we go on living, persisting.
Though united with cherubim and seraphim, their song
of praise has no earth under it, the severed dream
of the old meets here the young people's longing
to reverberate with meaning, their blue or green
painted eyelids beneath headscarves, almond eyes bright
by the icon of St Michael with its wax *i.v.*,
brown and gold with reflected light.

Pastoral for Yet Another Christmas

Have I been sure, this Christmas-Eve,
God's own hand did the rainbow weave
Whereby the truth from heaven slid
Into my soul?
               Robert Browning

Norway's at war, though only one percent, tops,
which means we're at least ninety-nine percent at peace
this Christmas. Two dead and four wounded, when you stop
to think about it could be any Saturday night
when the wrong people mix their alcohol and steroids.
To our troops in and around Iraq, a Merry Christmas!
Stronger than iron and darkened green the pines
from Telemark stand in their helmets full of water,
sharp glitter falls, their medals fastened to their tips.
From the shop windows light cuts colder than the snow
among the city centre's heating coils and vents.
Oslo's expensive, but then everything is free,
blood tests, a morning paper, cell phone (although there's
a catch, in that case), free admittance and a drink.
The African lady back there in the waiting room
who from her stretcher sent out a time-capsule tube
of blood looked like she'd gotten rid of something evil
and now, between the holidays, could take a breather.
All things are resting in a natural harmony,
but there's no nature in my neighbourhood to speak of,
now all of the aquatic life is crystalised
in brittle tines hung from the mudguards of the bikes,
and untouched shells of white snow over rust-dark cars,
and the communal cat who, soon as she is fed,
evaporates, part too of biologic life,
along with the sea scallops packed into my freezer.
Yes, this, our Earth, is a blue, shimmering star of ice,

and in due time the Christmas peace will find me, too,
from the high ceiling of this subdivided flat.
My daughter pines for Father Christmas and her pining
becomes its own time-space, a festival, an island,
a secret life of courtly, awkward ceremony,
and waiting, mostly, like the long breaks on a film set.
Christmas Eve, soon, in my divorced state, on the table
glasses stand waiting in a waste space to be filled,
schnapps look like little fish mouths nipping at the surface
and deep-sea dark blue fills the balcony window.
In snowfall, glorious in spite of it all, falling
heavily on the city that we now call home:
Christmastime handed down, grown new, in celebration
of Odin's theft, and of the star above the stall.

ODE TO THE DEMIURGE

Ode till demiurgen, 2013

Spring Evening. Shipping Out.

'Comme je descendais des Fleuves impassibles…'
                                        Rimbaud

i

These frigates, cutters, quick-scudding slender vessels,
come Saturday about to put out on the night's
immense, suspenseful freedom, fleeing house arrest,
now loud beside the bright, blank waters, and tempestuous
with cigarettes as yet unlit and paper-white,
blankly unwritten, in their lips, fast ships – small, light.
I see them from my dead calm, so forlorn and worn,
though they mistake my gaze, in the night trolley's corner,
hair lank as spring rain tied back, scarves, black round their eyes,
their slim arms crabwise on the rail as they careen
this way then that upon the Sea of Puberty;
they stand, baskets in hand, in food-marts in the evenings
and see my gaze but cannot fathom that it means
I'm seven and am seeing my sister at sixteen,

ii

her scarf of the same type, her miniskirt as tight,
leaving port forever as she goes aboard,
the young blood restless, ready to risk it all outright.
How Top of the Pops is off the air and heavy music
is rolling, heeling over as it courses forward,
breaking the wave's crest, the prow seething with white foam.
With a whole generation and all ships underway
where the same key has opened up a high blue dome
and every tipsy boat goes laughing over the reef.
How she, whom I admire, for some time looks on me

with a pained tenderness of sorts, who still am safe
in my old world; some of you quickly come to grief,
some sail on, and with not a scar upon its face
the sea is nonetheless crossed by the paths you've lost.

iii

With boats that put out and perpetually sail forth
I associate each new spring dress and daring heel.
You glide out, and the circle's edge expands once more
around the midpoint with its fluttering vintage coat.
Decked out and painted up, the girls stand undelivered,
fit to burst, eager at the bowsprits of their boats
for evening to begin, with its rewards, its risks.
Soon scarless sea, unsentimentally oblivious,
you lightly glide along the ocean's polished disk,
an evening round together, not allowed ashore
yet, wobbly, groping your way forward, now dishevelled,
tipsy, and shouting from the railings of your vessels
such secret words as, apprehended in the port,
are recognised as common, trivial expressions.

The Stairs

(Psalm 23:5)

I've been imploring you so long to come
the day's imprinted in red, in a heart shape.
Cancel at this stage? Never! Sooner succumb
to my pneumonia than put off our date.
Today June's blinding, with the kitchen's windowpanes
roundly fulfilled with greenery and brimming sun.

It takes me a good hour to get into my clothes
and grocery shopping in the unmoved summer air
is heavy as swimming in a sea of gasoline.
It's morning, yet I'm half-passed out standing in line
with this painstakingly selected angler fish,
of seven on display the one with the ugliest mug
and thus the most delicious, its black gaze stiff
and glassy as my own is thanks to my high fever.
A taxi home, all the way up the stairs I'm wheezing.
My sacrificial victim watches me in the kitchen,
its dead eyes giving back my mirror image.
I force myself to stand, everything is prepped,
filet it, cut up a whole form's worth of the fish,
which leaves a good bit over to stow away in the fridge.
The batter's on the table, my shirt's heavy with sweat,
heart pounding heavy, carefully whipped, thick
lemon sauce with sifted flour, garlic, ginger
and, sprinkled on a bed of white rice, black-brown wild rice.
My fever boils up in the kitchen's fragrant cloud
of hot frying oil, with the blood coursing in a ring
on the inside, where now the house's finest china,
with a dessert chock-full of sweetness, is laid out.
Pastries and little cakes, After Eights, chocolate truffles
I catch my gay neighbour eyeing covetously.
Up on the top floor, in the communal kitchen,
the love feast is laid out, a panoply of riches
from land and sea, angler in lemon sauce, raw rice
scattered with pitted dates, the ambrosial bouquet
of rosé from a glass you'll drink from with such care
with painted red lips, such variety it's as if
I'd killed a bull myself and gutted him to prepare
this sumptuous fare, like my own flesh and blood
squeezed from the time prior to my hospital visit.
My own delicious, wicked nature lying there

on offer, say, in place of Sister Angler Fish.
At the new moon, so no menstruation will postpone
my sly love's full communion, ruining the feast.
The doorbell sounds its mediated tone.
I hurl myself down the stairs, pulse rate doubled due
to my 104-degrees fever, fall to my knees
at last, collapse from sheer exhaustion, sprawling prone
there at the threshold, yes, I lie down, I am done.
In the door, lovely as all I've ever hungered for,
you stand, looking like you have painted on those shorts,
your red lips smiling, albeit a bit doubtfully,
high overhead this man lying here down and out
at your feet, by the first step, the very first one,
no more than that, forgive me how I've fallen short.
Oh praise be unto you, munificent creation,
so plainly beyond my power to participate in.
Against my fevered brow the evening air is good.
Above us, the feast, already served, is growing cold.
The bouquet stands, its stems slender as little children.
A still flame flutters from the candles in their holders,
throwing violet shadows up and down the walls' dry wood.
An evening service on a peak I can't ascend,
out of reach, now, for me, lying on the ground floor,
with the stairs over me, and yet there is a blessing,
this mild June evening, in each object of perception,
a shaded, moist garden where, rolling onto my back,
I see the roses rising out of fertiliser
to climb the high vines, purely for the sake of you,
along the gables; a quartz-studded gravel path
swaying a little, a drop of moisture from the grass
that trembles on the shining black strap of your shoe,
this drop the last thing before darkness falls. Upstairs
the table waits with burning candles, empty chairs.

Closing Time and Cleanup

Finally life has opened you up deep within me,
    your heart beating with love to every last detail,
to the silk strand of hair upon that woman's shank
    through fishnet, to each hennaed hair upon her head,
to the bell round the falcon's neck, its silver sound,
    to the boy's proud look in his soccer uniform
passing by on this soft blue evening in early fall,
    to the mosquito's wing, to the small globe of blood
on her proboscis, as warm and good as the blood was
    at birth around my temples, down around my ears,
round as our Earth's blue smoothness after storms.
    First upon coming home does Darwin in his heart
see how among the islands' solidly rounded forms
    the daring colours and designs go wandering
in mandalas far different from the stiff equations
    of a Linnaeus, and suddenly ice-cold he sobs beneath
a streetlight, awestruck at the kingdom of this world.
    With every particle they sweep into the dustpan
my parched mouth will be heard now to proclaim your praises.
    Yes, each one of my atoms will reach out to its neighbour
as to a friend and give thanks that at length I came
    here to this coast of life's streetlight-illumined evening.
The crossword puzzle that the waitress solved completely
    and left behind her found you by your every name.

After the Concert

i

At a felafel place submerged in snow last evening
the neon of the window sign not constituting
a focused object for my thoughts and ill-conceived
generalizations vis-à-vis the past and future,
when, broad-hipped, overweight, a mother with her three
downy-haired little hard-rockers came traipsing in,
Slayer t-shirts worn on top from the concert just concluded
around the corner. The kids are happy, in a spin,
Oh that was huge! The speared kebab is spinning, too,
for the daughter's boyfriend with his long, hard-rocker hair,
for the daughter, blade-thin, for the son, behind whose trace
of moustache a soft mouth tries hard to hide from view.

ii

He smiles, embarrassed, his ears deafened, *south of heaven*,
with happiness that's still a child's, with youthful grace,
with mottled grey-blue eyes someone will someday find
strong, safe. And in the ebbing ecstasy the place
encloses, before we are scattered, I note signs
in the mum's round forms of the punk rock era lingering,
whatever that means now, now that thirty or so
anonymous long years have been extinguished
out in the suburb they'll soon drive to. Strings of slow
oxygen bubbles surface behind the bright glass.
Evident are her thoughtfulness and self-control,
and what it's cost to keep their little craft afloat.

iii

I wonder what you'd make of these notations
about to push off and head home, while I just hang,
all of the onions on my plate, still, the tomatoes,
too, like in childhood – that much, anyway, hasn't changed,
athough the time's been used up. Outside, the remains
of the Norwegian working class in overcoats
and some kind of pyjama-like sweatsuits, one gang
laughing, sky-high, at a sign on the convenience store,
the falling snow. And others closing time lures forth –
Somalis with their purple lips in outer darkness.
Enchanted words, still. Slush, splashes from passing cars,
all this seen from amidships. I remain on board.

The Trash Pile

When you tell stories from the years spent in Alaska,
about that sojourn with an Indian tribe you had,
I feel a fraction of my old enthusiasm
for the aboriginal and primeval coming back.
It seems that they had everything a man could ask for:
the most advanced appliances, the latest flat screens.
But as for sanitation... The whole tribe had to track
out to a central midden to take care of that,
houses around them in a ring, sticking their asses
out at the pile's round slope; it wasn't all that bad
in fall and spring, but the cold stung you like small daggers
in winter and in summer the stench made you gag,

on bright nights that lured the whole local population
of beryl-blue and beer-bottle-glass green metallic
flies to the light of your softly bulbous white lamp.
Forgive me, love, it's just that I can actually see it
before me, your red lips and nails eleven fast points
of colour in that oceanic light's abstraction.
Backlit, the trash heap glittering with its bottle glass,
with bones the dogs as yet can't wrench loose sticking out
as if they were the armoured horns of a great dragon
that has been slumbering beneath the logged-out forests.
It sighs with exhalations and evening, spasms passing
through it. A wyrm, a tragic creature dreaming half-
awake, its green eyes made of bottle-bottoms' glass,
its body of plastic, car parts, animal cadavers.
The salmon harvest strands here, and mussel shells, perhaps,
if not just chicken nuggets from a gold mine run
by our all-powerful, global conglomerate or one
of its subsidiaries – as here the last Indians
watched cable and drank beer. Though when it comes to that,
all I have actual experience of is the trash pile,
not the canoes by the Pacific Ocean, dragged
up at day's end and filled with summer daylight practically
undiminished when as evening light it gleams.
The trash pile towers over the surrounding flatlands
following a curved stretch of coastline, and it seems
to me to stretch along with the meridians
from Pole to antipode, at the world's top from white
calotte to dark blue coast, under an airy sphere.
Your shimmering orb, Lord of this world: now the earth shines,
and the trash pile, listen how it ferments like wine,
in glory, welfare bound for the celestial port.
It shines: waste, metal, and bones with muscle fibres
of microchips' spider veins along the circuit boards.
Our world's luxurious trash, Lord, to your honour here:

the core industrial waste, soft parts on the outside,
organically composted, smoke and vapours hung
above the trash pile, arching like the planet curves
along the bends of the Pacific's edge and tongue.
The shadings billowing across the mountain slopes
in late light pass the ocean and the pile, shifting
form and colour as if their praises were being sung.
A trash heap in a wasteland, shimmering still
with the pine forests' phosphor-green and sea's chrome-blue,
a tract where evening light is delicately flung
down with the angel to this demarcated dump.
A Zion both of swarming life and of decay,
a motley multiplicity doomed to waste away.
A place where you can see the whole sky at one time,
briskly chill, and widely eye each diamond cut
detail of the globe's day that hurries on its way.
What can I call you, dismal pile, who sparkle when
a ray of light falls where you show yourself as soiled
as this, in this stench, all our expectations spoiled.
You dream in vain of the cocoon's emancipation,
for what higher purpose and meaning continuing to live,
with only spasms standing in for the resurrection
deep in the interior's seething fermentation,
and seeing only with swarms of compound insect eyes
mosquitoes and bluebottles in cloud formation circling
around you in a dusk that lasts the whole night through.
Midsummer soon and far up in the blue meridians
a sordid trash pile craves a benediction, too.
Up from the lowest level it perpetually stretches,
Lord, and it lauds unto its last breath your creation.

NEW POEMS

2014–2016

'After the Rain'

to accompany the painting by Merete Løndal

At the round tables a new ruling class,
they kick at the dog-like shadow where it lies
beneath the tablecloth in chalk-white light.
The grappa stream is thin but burns as bright
as sunlight through a magnifying glass.
It's Sunday or a dead election day.
Facets of light glittering on the whirlpool
that sink perspective like a fishing line
in a deep well of memory dark and cool
have been perceived by those processing past
headed to lunch. All of that old class hatred
is admiration, now, for the ones who've made it,
if not one's peer, exactly, a twin, a mate –
no but a likely kidney donor if later
the evening traffic slips up, as it might.
On each table in turn, each desert isle,
wine glasses seem filled up with milk by the waiter's
white serving jacket fluttering past
that soon enough will bear behind their backs
a blood-red vintage to their dentally dazzling
toasts in one of the EU languages,
in which the truly sensitive palate senses
a drop of the old wolf's blood that's been tamed
by the sly foxes of our new consensus.

Words for Justyna on Her Departure for a Retreat in Tushita

Regina Derieva in mente

i

This world that you see, Justyna, really exists.
    a stone's a stone, even the thought behind
your temporal bone, while of a veil-like thinness,
    is not a dream or watery mirror image.
Your occipital lobe in the travel-pillow's grip
    receives the TV picture in space and time.
The meditation awaiting you in Tushita
    at Dharmasala in the Dali Lama's exile
can't change the fact that everything unwinding
    around you will be hard and soft and tactile.
The world you see is in no sense a fiction
    hit upon by your six senses, and this
in spite of the Rinpoche's proven mediation,
    while the blue sky arching above you will
continue most definitively still
    not to have you or your gaze for its origin,
the vegetation on mountain ridges to differ
    insignificantly for the other visitors
who sit immediately beside you, quiet
    as mice, in the same uncomfortable position.

ii

You bow your lovely neck to Asia
    and mildly reprimand our deficits,
our individualism and self-interest,

but Europe doesn't need to seek remission
in talk of tantric energy and the right
    balance of masculine and feminine.
How can I best reply? Between us two,
    the attraction and significance you hold
for me lie not in your bright womanhood,
    but spring from the invisible ground plan
you as an individual are founded on.
    Personality free as Shelley's west wind,
spun like a spider's web, ingeniously intricate,
    more wide-ranging by far in its cognition
than the inquiring needle of the compass is,
    out from the blood-dark labyrinth
where it has been unspinning it looks, blinking
    with your twin blue eyes in the midday light,
up from the subway, at the bar over a drink,
    a face, your own, singular and distinct.

iii

Europe exalts the spirit like a gothic spire
    and pines in exile for lost paradise.
We are not here to look upon our lives
    as drunken bondages to be despised.
Tell rinpoche and guru that from me.
    The individual's freedom to decide is
prismatically composite and thousand-sided,
    you are not a representative in my eyes
for some great cosmic drama's rounded *yin*,
    a complement in anonymous two-sidedness.
What do I care for Eve's or Lilith's tribes,
    the cow in the herd, udders dripping into

bucket and bottle and collective when I
　　can share with you one moment liberated
from time's streaming continuum?
　　For me you are as irreplaceable, finally,
as our brief, rain-whipped instant
　　now here an early spring without repetition,
and without precedent, new, short-lived,
　　in an eternally sunny Buddha's grin.

　　iv

Your thought, real, with reality's full width
　　in hand and within reach, its prism
of content-rich, personal variation
　　of free initiative, and with our tradition
linking us up to Bach's architectonics
　　and Dante's rising and revolving spiral.
Your thought, when it attains complexity,
　　has touched God's, growing brighter in its climb,
the seraphs singing, then, your thought in its circle –
　　isn't this too a lotus meditation?
The formal beauty of the planets aligned in
　　conjunction, isn't this an insight into
a deep harmony equally dignified?
　　It's in a mortal body God is made man,
not motionless at a mandala's midpoint.
　　In the clear light of an agonizing Christ
heaven falls, while directly under him
　　on the ground, soldiers are seen casting dice
and the timber of the cross is just as true
　　as the spirit moving over still waters.

v

What I resist is the view according to which
    heaven and hell are no more than inner visions,
projected on a world outside to bind
    together all its shimmering apparitions.
The victim dies two times, then, and the crime's
    a dream, a cosmic comedy of some kind.
The black SS-battalion soon turns white,
    to snow or ashes, or, in another likeness,
to ice-glazed clay blown out in the blink of an eye,
    black candles on a cake with white icing,
and everything they're teaching there in India
    to empty forms in an unending ring.
Two death's-head epaulettes that sunken lie
    in a snow drift, in abstract, depersonalised
karma? Lovely, but nothing one could live by.
    No, every strand of hair will stand inscribed
like the twelve-year-old Jewish girl's cry.
    For what good can the spirit, left behind,
ever do, when, as we have seen, it
    can scarcely shift a dinner plate an inch?

vi

It's in the body the soul's become incarnate
    and – a picture of controlled sensibility –
can steer its stream of impressions and intellect;
    no, let them fly, high on the wing
of their own motion. Tell me, does a rose stink,
    and does a lark live hidden in a slippery
dark hole? Returned from his retreat, the enlightened
    yogi is skin and bones, in pitiful condition.

What does he have to tell you about this life
　　spread out on all sides, you, your I, in the middle?
In spite of all my faults, which are conspicuous
　　enough, I am prepared to here bear witness
that you are entirely pure, your rosy limbs,
　　your sweat is clean to me, even your pee is,
each smoothly executed function annexed
　　by your personality, where every action
performed in this world is a sketch that hints
　　at life eternal, and not some thin illusion.
A life that's written down in your hand's lines,
　　unique as the snow flake that a single time
falls

TRANSLATOR'S AFTERWORD

Far from being merely decorative, Håkan Sandell's metres and rhymes are essential to his poems, as necessary as a skeleton to a vertebrate animal. I've therefore chosen to follow the example of Richard Wilbur in his brilliant translations from French, Spanish, Russian – and any other language he turns his hand to – who has said that he tries 'to be as slavish as is consistent with being imaginative and lively'. Happily, Sandell himself advocates this approach. His most common criticisms of the drafts I have shown him was not that they were inaccurate, but that I hadn't captured enough of the original's verse music, that they didn't sufficiently *swing*. I hope that the translations included in the present volume do, when all is said, swing.

The job is made easier by the fact that Swedish, like English, is a Germanic language, and that the same systems of versification are historically established in the two languages. Sandell, one of the chief agents of the renewal of metrical poetry in Swedish, nearly always writes either in a strong-stress metre adapted from Germanic *knittelvers* – that is, rhymed lines with four strong stresses in each line – or in iambic pentameter or hexameter. Iambic pentameter is ubiquitous in English, and arguably more natural than in Swedish, while strong-stress, or accentual, verse appears in English in modern contexts as diverse as Eliot's *Four Quartets* and rap music. Iambic hexameter, or the *alexandrine*, after the French twelve-syllable line, has never really caught on in English, but was popular in Sweden from the Baroque period, when it was introduced from France, up to the end of the National Romantic period in the 1920s. Sandell generally employs the mid-line caesura typical of the form, while allowing himself more frequent metrical substitutions in conjunction with it, and varying its exact placement more than was traditionally the case.

Sandell has expanded the resources of Swedish rhyme more than any other poet in the past hundred years: first, by including, along with full rhyme, assonantal, or vowel rhyme, often in combination with consonance; second, by stringing out threads of such assonances that go on, sometimes literally, for pages. For examples see 'To a Young Man Who Arrived at the Party Dressed in a Lady's Fur', 'To a Female Friend Travelling in Thailand', and, in particular, the final poem, 'Words for Justyna on Her Departure for a Retreat in Tushita', in which nearly all of the poem's 120 lines terminate in one of two vowel sounds. In addition to full and assonantal end-rhyme, Sandell is partial to frequent internal rhyme, influenced as he is by Old Norse and medieval Welsh verse forms, and by the theories and practice of the Baroque Swedish Poet George Stiernhielm. The result, as I hope the reader will be able to judge even in translation, is a verse music very much Sandell's own, at once improvisatory and incantatory.

In the poems where Sandell works in received forms – the quatrains from 'Stanzas to the Spirit of the Age' and the *terza rima* of 'A Summer in the Hood' – the rhymes are typically more exact, and, in the case of the latter poem in particular, I've been helped by the example of Derek Walcott's daring rhyming beginning with *Midsummer* (1984), an important volume for Sandell.

NOTES

THE EVIL ONE (p. 23)

'The Evil One' begins on page thirteen of the volume in which it originally appeared.

Elemental: a nature spirit.

Homunculus: A small, artificially-created human. In *De natura rerum* (1537), Paracelsus recommends: 'that the sperm of a man be putrefied by itself in a sealed cucurbit for forty days with the highest degree of putrefaction in a horse's womb, or at least so long that it comes to life and moves itself, and stirs, which is easily observed. After this time, it will look somewhat like a man, but transparent, without a body. If, after this, it be fed wisely with the Arcanum of human blood, and be nourished for up to forty weeks, and be kept in the even heat of the horse's womb, a living human child grows therefrom, with all its members like another child, which is born of a woman, but much smaller' (cited in *Promethean Ambitions: Alchemy and the Quest to Perfect Nature*. William Newman, 2004).

Nephilim: offspring of a human and an angel, a union that typically produced giants, rather than dwarves. See the extra-canonical *Book of Enoch*.

THE ASSAULT (p. 28)

Wer hat dich so geschlagen... First line of a stanza in J. S. Bach's *Johannes Passion* and *Matthäus-Passion*, originally stanza three of 'O Welt, sieh hier dein Leben' ('O world, see here your life') by Paul Gerhardt (1607–1667):

> Wer hat dich so geschlagen,
> mein Heil, und dich mit Plagen
> so übel zugericht'
> du bist ja nicht ein Sünder
> wie wir und unsre Kinder,
> von Missetaten weißt du nicht.

Who is it that hath bruised Thee?
Who hath so sore abused Thee
And caused Thee all Thy woe?
While we must make confession
Of sin and dire transgression,
Thou deeds of evil dost not know.

(trans. John Kelly)

NEW JEANS (p. 44)

Salubrin: Swedish brand of disinfectant. From the Latin *salubris*, healthful.

The Army and Navy: In the original, *Arbetarboden*, literally 'worker's shop', a type of store specializing in affordable blue-collar work clothes.

Engelbrektsgatan: common street name in Sweden, here referring to a shopping street in the old town of Malmö. Engelbrekt Engelbrektsson (1390–1436) led an unsuccessful rebellion against Erik of Pomerania, king of the united kingdoms of Denmark, Norway, and Sweden. From the German, meaning 'bright or glorious angel'.

ICE. DARKNESS. (p. 49)

Audhumbla: in Norse myth, the primeval cow. She lived by licking salty blocks of ice, and in the process uncovered Búri, the first of the gods, and the grandfather of Odin.

XMAS. KRUSE STREET, OSLO. (p. 50)

Original title 'X-mas. Krusesgate.'

Krusesgate: a street in Oslo. Two old patrician houses on the street were turned into squats for most of the 1990s.

half-way: Dante was thirty-five at the beginning of his journey, half-way through the traditional span of years allotted to human beings. In the volume in which the poem originally appeared (*Sketches for a Century*) this line falls at the bottom of p. 34. The poem begins on p. 33. According to tradition, Christ died aged thirty-three.

SKETCHED IN THE MARGIN. OSLO IN JUNE. (p. 51)

Michael: the Danish poet Michael Strunge (1958–1986), a friend of Sandell's.

diamatic: an abbreviation of 'dialectical materialism'.

Rudolf Nilsen (1901–1929): Norwegian socialist poet, dead of tuberculosis by age twenty-eight. Raised in Oslo in the Tøyen/Grønland neighbourhood of Oslo where the poem is set.

TWENTY-TWO THINGS NOT TO BE TRUSTED... (p. 57)

Hávamál, meaning *Sayings of the High One*, is a series of Old Norse poems from the Viking Age. Sections 85 and 86 consist of the following list of things to watch out for:

85.

A snapping bow, a burning flame,
A grinning wolf, a grunting boar,
A raucous crow, a rootless tree,
A breaking wave, a boiling kettle,

86.

A flying arrow, an ebbing tide,
A coiled adder, the ice of a night,
A bride's bed talk, a broad sword,
A bear's play, a prince' s children...

(trans. W. H. Auden and Paul Taylor)

Mikael Wiehe (1946–): Swedish singer-songwriter, whose works include a song in praise of Stalin ('Sången om Stalin') recorded by the band Knutna Nävar (Clenched Fists) in 1973. Wiehe was at the time a member of the Hoola Bandoola Band, whose 1972 album was entitled *Vem kan man lita på* (*Who Can You Trust?*).

I DON'T TOLERATE ALCOHOL SO WELL ANY LONGER... (p. 58)

Vaterland: from the Dutch, meaning 'watery ground'. A section of Oslo known for its inexpensive drinking places.

THE BOGOMILES... (p. 60)

Bogomiles: Christian sect that flourished in Bulgaria from the tenth to as late as the seventeenth century, and more widely in the Byzantine Empire in the eleventh–twelfth centuries (*The Concise Oxford*

Dictionary of World Religions). Considered heretical by the church and vigorously persecuted.

vanitas: 'a seventeenth-century Dutch genre of still-life painting that incorporated symbols of mortality or mutability' (*OED*).

the soul in the infant returning: 'Euthymios Zigabenos in his *Panoplia* refers to the Bogomil belief in the resurrection of the dead body along with the demons that occupy the bones, a belief that is incompatible with the idea of reincarnation. Zigabenos, however, states that the Bogomils believe that their elect ones "do not die, but 'transmigrate'", as if in their sleep, painlessly divesting themselves of this clay vestment of flesh and dressing themselves with the indestructible and divine stole of Christ' ('Was There a Life Beyond the Life Beyond? Byzantine Ideas on Reincarnation and Final Restoration' Alexander Alexakis, 2001).

the age of the Spirit: Joachim of Fiore (c. 1135–1202) taught that history falls into three periods corresponding to the Father, Son and Holy Spirit. Sandell here elides Joachim's eccentric, though not heretical, vision of history with apocalyptic elements in Bogomilism.

PASTORAL FOR YET ANOTHER CHRISTMAS (p. 76)

Telemark: a mountainous, wooded inland region of Norway.

Odin's theft: Odin stole the mead of poetry from a giant and gave it to the gods. Mead was drunk (among many other times) at the midwinter festival that became associated with Christmas after Scandinavia was Christianised, and a dark, sweet *julöl* (Christmas beer) is still brewed at this time of year. Children are given *julmust*, a soda with a taste not dissimilar to that of the beer.

AFTER THE CONCERT (p. 86)

'South of Heaven' is the title track of a 1987 album by Slayer.

WORDS FOR JUSTYNA... (p. 94)

Rinpochen: honorific title meaning 'precious jewel'.